THE CYBER EFFECT

THE CYBER EFFECT

WHAT CAN YOU DO ABOUT IT?

RICK THOMAS

THE CYBER EFFECT:
What Can You Do About It?

ISBN 978-1-966741-03-9

Rick Thomas

Edited by Sarah Hayhurst

Life Over Coffee
8595 Pelham Rd Ste 400 #406,
Greenville, SC 29615
LifeOverCoffee.com

Dedication

Many of my thoughts were influenced by Mary Aiken's book, The Cyber Effect: An Expert in Cyber-psychology Explains How Technology Is Shaping Our Children, Our Behavior, and Our Values—and What We Can Do about It.

For additional resources, visit
lifeovercoffee.com

Table of Contents

Introduction

Technology, social media, and the Internet can be redemptive instruments in the hands of individuals who want to do good and know how to accomplish those positive purposes practically. Of course, the implication in a fallen world is clear: technology in the hands of someone who does not have redemptive values can disrupt and do harm to their souls and those around them. We all have stories of technology's misuse, which includes our tensions and temptations with social media, making it worth our time to ask the intrusive questions that might help us to consider more practically how to use technology redemptively. For example, What is the cyber effect of technology on your soul? Do you have a practical plan to guard against the potential problems associated with technology, the Internet, and social media?

No Ten Tech Tips

I will not share a list of tips about how to curb your tech habits, e.g., cut the Wi-Fi off at night or place password protection on your child's devices. That information is accessible to all of us. You may Google "ten helpful tips to [fill in the blank]" and find many options that will work for you. Each person and family is different, and I cannot speak to every individual or family dynamic. I recommend that you read what I have provided here, work through the questions, and then ask the Spirit of God to illuminate your mind about how to make specific, customized, practical applications to your life, family, and friends. What you need to do will be slightly different from me or your friends. Take this material seriously and be pneumatic; God will meet you at the level of your determination to change.

My goal is to challenge you about why you must address technology and social media use. If I cannot convince you why the cyber effect is potentially damaging to your soul and most crucial relationships, you probably will not carry through with whatever your "tech tips" happen to be. It would be like giving a person a workout routine for the gym because it's the new year and they are going through their "annual conviction" to make a change. If the unhealthy person does not believe their health is on the line, their long-term motivation to change will run out of steam by the end of January. My prayer is that we will go deeper than behavioral modification, as needful as that is (Matthew 5:30), as the Lord captures our hearts (Romans 8:13) regarding this cultural contagion. If He does this for us, it will be the perfect spot to start thinking about how to apply good tech habits to our lives.

When It Changed

Circa 1450, Johannes Gutenberg introduced the printing press to the world. Many people consider this event to be one of the most transformative inventions of the second millennium. His "moveable type machine" changed lives, cultures, and countries. Though books were already in print, the printing press made information accessible and brought people together for good and evil. In 2007, Steve Jobs gave us the mobile phone, which will go down in history as one of the high points of this millennium. Though the Internet was already here with its technologies, it was not until the iPhone that the culture sped up and changed exponentially. The pre-existing "handheld wannabes" were nice, but the iPhone made us cool—and craving for more. Some statisticians estimated in 2018 that over 5 billion people had mobile devices, and over half own smartphones. That number has grown since. Nearly every family you know has at least one smartphone, if not more. Upward to 80 percent of homes in developed countries have personal computers.

But before I go dark about the dangers of devices, let me state clearly that we all benefit from technology. I'm not here to suggest it's an utterly lousy idea, a big fail, and you should run from it. We have testimonies about the good things the Lord has done through technology. I'm not tossing the baby out with his iPhone. Our tech-dependent culture has been a positive advancement on all fronts, e.g., health services, financial institutions, academic environments, and businesses. When we began developing our business model in 2008, the over-arching question was, "How can we use technology redemptively? How can we take the gospel's good news to the world?" We understood there was an "echo of omnipresence" in technology, and we hoped to capitalize on this means of grace for God's glory and the transformative benefit of millions (Matthew 5:45).

Over a decade later, the Lord has positioned us to wrap the globe daily. Our site is a "big box store in cyberspace." I call it our coffee shop or sanctification center. For example, we have a fully loaded Learning Management System (LMS) where we can train anyone in discipleship and biblical counseling if they have Internet access. They never have to leave their homes. We have millions of words in read, watch, and listen formats. You also have your lists of tech benefits for which you are grateful. You can shop online and wait for Amazon to appear on your doorstep. You don't have to purchase stamps because you can pay bills online. Some people do not carry money because of credit and debit cards. You can make transactions with your watch. The benefits are plenty, and more are coming. But with all good things that the Lord has given His creation (Matthew 5:45), there are tendencies and temptations to use them selfishly and cruelly (James 1:14-15).

Can't Study Fluid Events

One of the biggest problems with the Internet and technology is that you can't study it properly because it's an open-ended, ever-changing, fluid experience. The best studies happen after the event is over when you've had time to digest it, measure the results, look at patterns, and give a thorough review of what happened so you can prepare and protect yourself from repeating history, especially our evil history. For example, 9/11 is an open-and-shut tragedy in our country. We can study it because it's over. Thousands of research papers, books, forums, and boards figured out how we got to 9/11, how we responded to it, and its lingering effect. Pearl Harbor is another illustration of a study-able event. So is your childhood, as you reflect upon that closed period of your life to understand yourself more clearly. Once the event is over, you can begin collecting all the relevant data to see what you can learn about that unique historical phenomenon.

The Internet and technology are still active, fluid phenomena. We can't fully understand moving targets. Before the iPhone, we barely had time to fall in love with the iPod and its walloping impact on the music industry. Then came the iPad, which begged for social media platforms like Facebook, and YouTube, which used to be a thing with the teens, but they jumped to Instagram, Snapchat, TikTok, and beyond. Like frogs on lily pads, we're jumping from one technological pond to the other at the speed of the Internet. Technology changes, new habits form, and we're still trying to understand the effects of the last cool thing that we had to have. It will take at least another twenty years, if not longer, to figure out what we did to ourselves. But that does not mean we don't know things today. Though technology changes, the habits and their effects are somewhat measurable. The challenge for us will be if we do not allow what we already know to persuade us to change how we think about and use technology.

Technology Reveals Us

I have interacted with thousands of people of every age, and technology has adversely affected them—to some degree. Some of them know it. Others do not. Some care. Others do not. The big idea for us to understand at this juncture is how the adverse effects of technology are symptoms, not the cause of our problems. James was forthright when he taught us that sin is not "out there somewhere" but in our hearts, making the effect of technology the thing that highlights our hearts. Listen to our brother: "But each person is tempted when he is lured and enticed by his own desire. Then desire when it has conceived gives birth to sin, and sin when it is fully grown brings forth death" (James 1:14-15). Jesus was more succinct when He said, "Out of the abundance of the heart, the mouth speaks" (Luke 6:45). James and Jesus quickly tied the external phenomenon— technology—to our hearts, the source of our problems. The iPhone, for example, reveals what's happening in my heart, the things I crave.

James and Jesus want you to know that the primary problem is not technological but how these devices and platforms reveal the pre-existing conditions in our souls. If our hearts did not desire it, technology would not be able to lure us. A device is "just a device," but if we crave it, we permit it to manage us; what you need will control you. For example, I'm not too fond of mayonnaise. I've never enjoyed the taste of it. It's not a spiritual thing at all. It's a taste thing. If I were to wallow in a pool of mayonnaise, there would be zero temptation to taste it or become addicted. The upside to this inside truth about our hearts craving the things of the world, even to our detriment, is that we can take the measure of an adult, child, or friend by the things they love. Their treasure reveals their hearts. When you see how much technology affects an individual practically, you get a snapshot of who they are internally. Here are a few illustrations.

- The lady who has ongoing selfie shots as you scroll through her Facebook profile is revealing her heart. In no real-life context would she break out her photo album and show you twenty iterations of herself—unless she was a narcissist.
- The child sequestered off in his room who does not socialize with his family reveals his heart. He is making a value statement about himself and those closest to him.
- The couple that goes on a date and stares at their phones testifies to everyone in the restaurant what they think of each other. Rather than dating another person, they bring their phones and "talk to their devices."
- When someone in a meeting with you checks their buzzing phone, they make a value statement about you. We teach our kids not to interrupt us because it's not respectful. But we permit our phones to interrupt us.
- A dad comes home from a long day at work and clicks on the TV or jumps on the Internet, a tablet, or a phone. Rather than engaging his family in real space, he zips off to cyberspace, leaving his family behind eating his cyber-dust.

In these illustrations, there is always a "yes, but exception," some of which are valid. But if that is our first impulse, we're defending ourselves too quickly while missing the point, which could speak to where we are with all of this (Matthew 7:3-5).

Call to Action

1. Why do you need a device? I'm asking a need question, not a desire question. Needing something is more potent than merely desiring it. For example, you desire ice cream but don't need it.
2. What are five positive reasons you need technology, social media, and the Internet?
3. What are five negative reasons you desire technology, social media, and the Internet?
4. Will you discuss the five negative reasons with someone you trust, who will speak candidly with you?
5. What one thing will you change about how you use the Internet, technology, and social media, aiding you to become more like Christ?

1

Real World Effect

There is a discussion about whether cyberspace is real or not. We know what a real, tactile place is, but what is cyberspace? You can't touch or taste it. Is it real? If you were to make a case for cyberspace being real, how would you steel man your position? The arguments are compelling on both sides, but there is a more straightforward way to cut through the debate. The next time someone is on their phone, converse with them. Are they "with you" or somewhere else, regardless of how you define that other place? As texting and driving have proven in dramatic and horrific ways, you are somewhere else when you're on your phone. You have been behind that person at the traffic light as you "patiently" waited for them to get off their phones so everyone could continue their day. Most folks understand that you can't do two things simultaneously well. Regarding technology, if it's in front of you, whoever else is with you is the second fiddle.

Technology not only isolates us in our cyber-chambers, but it speeds us up, creating fast-paced mindsets that trick us into thinking that we must accomplish more, faster. There is no desire to eliminate hurry from our lives as we calculate which line in the store is moving more quickly so we can get in it to gain that precious extra two seconds. After we pick our line, we must leave the building before the person behind us who chose the other line. (Perhaps

I'm only speaking to the men here.) We park close to the door to get in and out quickly because time is valuable. Our tech addiction is imperceptible as our minds leave the natural world and those relationships, preoccupying us with the tyranny of the urgent. Those who build these platforms and devices understand our idolatries as they gamify their machines to entice the unaware. We eagerly watch the dots bubble up, waiting to see what's coming from cyberspace as our real-world relationships wait for us to return.

Distraction and distance from others are the death knell to personal holiness and redemptive relationships. Then there is the sabotaging of our memory banks. Nothing sticks if more than one thing competes for our minds' dominance. Our sanctification suffers; our relationships do not mature, and the zeitgeist wins the battle for our brains. Sitting still, being patient, waiting our turn, making eye contact, and enjoying a long-form, undistracted conversation with a friend is from an era when folks had the time to sit on the porch, enjoy the sunset, and build a lasting relationship with a spouse, family member, friend, or neighbor. Today, our front porches are small and barren places to plop our pumpkins, and our back decks are huge with grills as we isolate from folks while drifting off to cyberspace.

Call to Action

1. Is cyberspace a real place or not? What are your arguments to support your position?
2. What happens when you're talking to someone and their phone buzzes? Do they stay with your conversation, or do they break off to respond to the buzz?
3. Do you habitually respond to your phone when it beckons, even when conversing with someone? If so, what would be a better practice?
4. Will you talk to a family member about your relationship with them and your devices? How have you affected them—negatively or positively—with your technology practices?
5. What one tech change will you implement to slow down and eliminate hurry from your life?

2

Identity Effect

One of the most potent effects of the second fiddle phenomenon happens in a child's life when he grows into an adult. The young teen is transitioning from kid to adult. He's different in every way. It's a frightful time for many of these children. Their bodies are changing. They're starting to sound different. Their desires and habits are changing. They look different and are insecure as they begin to wonder who they are. The transitioning child significantly depends on others at this crucial age regarding identity formation. He measures those around him to see if they approve or disapprove of him. The opinions of other people have a transforming impact on how he thinks of himself. The family is his most potent shaping influence in helping him think biblically about himself. For example, if the father is angry or distant, it will adversely impact the child's view of himself. The angry father makes a value statement about his child: "I don't like you." The passive dad says something similar: "You're not worthy of my attention."

An unstable marriage also fosters insecurity in the children as they try to cope with their parent's dysfunction. God created these children in His image, which comes with a "baked in the cake" desire for communal connection and acceptance. The Trinity is the divine, eternal community, and we are like them (Genesis 1:27). Teens want to benefit from the Imago Dei, which makes community and acceptance a crucial aspect to their ongoing maturity. These kids are only asking one question: "Will you accept me?" If the answer is "no," the child's identity will form around a presuppositional filter of rejection. If he is not benefiting from an accepting, loving community within his familial structure, social media platforms become the instant reflex for his unmet and legitimate desires. Ironically, central to all these platforms is the "like" button. The obvious point for the craving soul is that you can calculate other people's opinions of you by the number of "likes" you receive. Some will argue that they only check to see if the post or pic is popular. Please don't dismiss the subtleties of our evil hearts. This problem is what makes the selfie so tempting and dangerous. The primary point of the selfie is what it says about the person in the picture, the selfie-taker.

Once uploaded, the selfie-taker checks, rechecks, and checks again to see who liked the picture. Or, to state the issue more accurately, who liked them? The question is not primarily about liking the image but, "Will you like me?" The selfie is the vanity mirror in the bathroom moved to the public square, covertly asking you for your opinion of them, which you provide by your likes and comments. It's a warning to every parent, teacher, mentor, and other authority figure who influences a teen's life. Don't assume the Internet is innocuous or that your child is naive. Neither is true. The Internet is a "net" that captures souls. The Adamic tendencies of shame, guilt, and fear are active in every soul, including the struggling teen who is looking for someone to accept them. Suppose the teenager is part of a loving, encouraging, admonishing, and repenting family that trains him up biblically (Deuteronomy 6:4-9). This temptation will be minimal because he does not need other people or places to shape his identity. But it will be different for the child in a dysfunctional home, whose primary shaping influences are electronic devices and social media.

Call to Action

1. Why is the transitional period between childhood and adulthood so crucial? What happens to children physically and spiritually during this time?

2. As these kids transition, why must parents be there for them, helping them cross the great divide from child to adult?

3. How would a dysfunctional marriage or home motivate a child to find perceived safety in other places, and why is the Internet a likely candidate for refuge?

4. If your home has not been a haven of shalom and stability, what one change will you make to be a harbinger of peace and security?

5. Perhaps it would be wise to go to your child and discuss identity formation. If so, will you do it?

3

Stranger Effect

The teen is not the only struggling soul looking for a community. Sometimes, I will hear a person talk about how they met a stranger, and within minutes, they had an in-depth personal conversation with them. They glow about how easy and natural it was to talk. Then they say, "And he was a perfect stranger!" This interaction is called the "stranger on the train phenomenon." It's similar to the freedom and disinhibition in dating versus the rigors and risks of marriage. When a boy and girl meet and hit it off, they cannot stop talking to each other. They are tired at their day jobs because they have been chatting with each other most of the night. No limits exist to how much they talk and share on repeat. Engaging like this is easy if you have no history—grudges, unforgiveness, bitterness—with someone. There are no strangers at the bar, or it's like the conference speaker or blogger who is so transparent about his life.

Marriage is different from strangers on the train because "you brought him home with you" to live in a 24/7, unbreakable, lifetime relationship where sin abounds. You know them through and through. You know their tendencies and weaknesses. Their triggers. You have a historical record of all the times they have hurt you. It's two sinners in a box with no escape hatch. You are keenly aware of when or if you can be vulnerable with them. You're less willing to take a "communication risk" with them. Of course, there are unresolved issues that date back years. Neither of you has been good about confessing your sins to each other and asking for forgiveness. My point is that there are built-in risks with this kind of broken, albeit ongoing, relationship. But the stranger on the train? Refreshing! There are minimal risks, and you will never see them again after your next stop. The relationship reward is high, and the relationship risk is low. As we did while dating, we share freely and without fear.

Enter the Internet.

Cyberspace is the perfect place for strangers passing in the night. Because cyberspace is not a real place, but you can have—perceived—genuine relationships, you can benefit from what relationships offer without the downside of sin's fallenness. Those who come from broken families or dysfunctional marriages can be naive and craving enough to take their turn in cyberspace. It's like training wheels on a bicycle for the relationally weak, but the risks are higher than anyone perceives. It's addictive, drawing you in while keeping you from doing the hard work of building authentic relationships in the only world we have and where we cannot escape. It keeps the unwitting relationally immature while getting their fix minute-by-minute with their handheld devices.

Call to Action

1. Why would a child or teen talk to the "stranger on the train" before talking to their parents?
2. Why do freshly minted dating partners talk so much and married couples talk so little?
3. Why is it so hard to be vulnerable in long-term relationships where there has been past sin?
4. What is one benefit of keeping a clean slate with each other by confessing sins and transacting forgiveness?
5. Will you ask God for the courage to build real-world relationships and then begin that process by sharing with a close friend what you're learning here?

4

Disinhibition Effect

The concept of sharing freely and without fear is called the disinhibition effect. There is little inhibition about vulnerability with a stranger on the train because he can't hurt you, so you believe. Of course, the possibility of being vulnerable and lacking perceived risk is part of cyberspace's bait to lure us into its net. In real-world relationships, like our families or the local church, it's more challenging to "unlike" somebody. When bad things happen and hurts accumulate, we have to deal with them biblically (or not). How often have you read on Facebook that someone said something unkind and never confessed it as a sin or asked for forgiveness? Right! Me, either. It would be exceptional for Christians to clean up their cyber dustups on social media. The norm is a "hit and run" cyber collision because they don't have to interact with those annoying people in real life and space.

> Let no corrupting talk come out of your mouths, but only such as is good for building up, as fits the occasion, that it may give grace to those who hear. And do not grieve the Holy Spirit of God, by whom you were sealed for the day of redemption. Let all

bitterness and wrath and anger and clamor and slander be put away from you, along with all malice. Be kind to one another, tenderhearted, forgiving one another, as God in Christ forgave you.

(Ephesians 4:29-32)

The disinhibition effect releases us to say whatever is on our minds, and many times, we would never say those things to that person face-to-face. Real-world relationships take work, are tedious, and we offend people. That person who does not connect well in real space is a "Chatty Cathy" online. Why is she like this? She has had too much hurt in her real-world relationships, so before we judge her too quickly for lack of transparency in the real world, give this perspective a chance to simmer while thinking about how we can be a difference-maker in her life. Hurting souls are everywhere, especially in a local church. Perhaps their reasons for connecting online are defenseless, but they are reasons, nonetheless. Real life is strewn with broken people, while Facebook is full of folks who prefer false intimacy, as they put their best image forward while keeping everyone at "cyber-arms-length."

Social media is like a drug to the hurting, desperate soul. They want community, but the local community has burned them too many times to keep returning. They become Christian cynics in cyberspace. I use the drug analogy because that is what drugs do for the person with an addiction; they are looking for an escape to satiate a desire. They get high to get away from it all. The social media addict spends their time on the net—getting away from it all. It provides them with communal intimacy, albeit it's a false intimacy. I understand the temptation. It's like porn in that it's quick, accessible, and scratches an itch, but it does not come with the baggage and disappointment of fallen relationships. When a person embraces the disinhibition effect, they can unwittingly plunge into a darkness they never perceive while blaming everyone else for why they are doing what they are doing. They become victims with a portal and pathway to stay victimized.

Call to Action

1. What is the disinhibition effect, and why is it so relationally dangerous?
2. How do cyber relationships provide partial satiation to our Imago Dei communal desires?
3. What do porn and social media have in common when it comes to striving for relationship and the perceived satisfaction?
4. Have you succumbed to the disinhibition effect? If so, what is your first step in breaking free?
5. Is there someone you need to speak with because of something sinful you said to them online? If so, will you talk with them?

5

Sanctification Effect

After you meet the stranger on the train, and both of you throw inhibition to the wind, you may convince yourself that you're building a whole relationship with another person. You're not. At best, what you have is false intimacy; it's not the real thing. You cannot replicate and enjoy God's solution to companionship in cyberspace. "Then the Lord God said, 'It is not good that the man should be alone; I will make him a helper fit for him'" (Genesis 2:18). If you cut yourself off from all potential hurt, it's not possible to know God the way He wants you to know Him. You will carve out a world where you rely on yourself, building high walls and safe places. You won't be relying on the Lord (2 Corinthians 1:8-9), and the adverse effect of not engaging real people in the real fallen world is that the place you create will become a prison.

Sanctification is not safe. We're fallen people. Though cyberspace can incarcerate someone and keep the bad people away, it falls woefully short in the change process. You can do many things by yourself, but sanctification is not one of them. It takes a community. One of the implications of "sanctification" is "sinfulness." Without sin, there would be no need for progressive sanctification.

But there is sin; we should not ignore or run from it. We need to engage the sinfulness among ourselves so we can change. We must be in fallen, flesh and blood contexts where sin is apparent and unavoidable. We have to engage it, not "unlike" it. If you want to be a great baseball player, you need all of the components of baseball so you can learn the game. If you had no glove, for example, you would never understand the skills necessary to make it to the "bigs." In the world of fallen humanity, sin is vital to our transformation. But if we sequestered ourselves from fallen humanity, building a cyber refuge, we would not grow as we should. We need human beings if our hope is Christlikeness (John 17:17).

The other concern that centers on the sanctification effect and technology is that our thoughts need hibernation time to sink into our brains. This crucial aspect of sanctification means that the truth of God we want to absorb has to land and stick in our long-term memory banks. I'm not sure of a worse place to hinder this aspect of sanctification than the Internet and social media. You can test yourself. Think of the last ten quotes you liked on your favorite social media platform. You can't. Nobody can. Even if you could recall parts of them, they are on their way out your mental door because other "nuggets of the day" are waiting to roll in. If a fleeting thought, like, click, or picture were on one end of a spectrum and memorizing a verse or passage from the Bible was on the other, "liking" things on social media is closer to your fleeting thoughts than the rigors of memory work that sticks with you for years and brings sanctification transformation to your soul while enabling you to impact those around you redemptively.

Call to Action

1. Why can't you replicate and enjoy God's solution for companionship in cyberspace?

2. Why are hurt, disappointment, and other sins vital to our maturity? What happens if we cut ourselves off from these realities of fallenness?

3. Why do high walls and safe spaces feel right but are detrimental to our need to become Christlike?

4. How do the Internet and social media hinder our long-term memories, and why is this issue vital to our sanctification?

5. What one thing will you change to carve out downtime to practice pondering for extended periods, which teaches patience and perseverance?

6

Blue Light Effect

O ur lives operate on a twenty-four-hour cycle. You have observed how you become tired or drowsy at certain times of the day. Hopefully, that is in the evening, when your body tells you it's time to sleep. I used to become drowsy in the afternoons, but not so much now since making a few healthy adjustments. This cycle is God's mercy to us, so we will rest, refresh, and reboot with vigor to serve the Lord with all our hearts, minds, and strength. The Internet age is changing our rhythms. We're going from a well-ordered life to a chaotic one. One of the culprits is the blue light that comes from our devices. For example, in the evening, the melatonin levels in our bodies begin to rise, which signals our bodies to go to sleep. But if we spend the evening on a device, the blue light will "trick" us into thinking it's not bedtime; our melatonin levels drop like they would the following day when God's rays enter our rooms to wake us.

Disrupted sleep cycles result in the cyberspace cadet having difficulty sleeping, focusing, and paying attention. Of course, he will be tired at the wrong times, throwing him out of sync with others. The next day at school, he's disruptive or sleepy. He compromises his attention span, and his agitation levels can rise. Sadly, one of the typical "remedies" for the kid who needs a jolt to stay alert in school is medication. It has become our impulse to take him to a counselor because we want our child to achieve an optimal outcome, even if we have to drug him to get there. At that juncture, to the non-discerning eye, he falls into the black hole of disorders. He's labeled! A secular counselor does not look for source causes but symptoms that align with the DSM-5-TR nomenclature, their descriptive psychology book. If the child's behavior matches a certain number of descriptions in the DSM, he receives a label, forming his identity.

It's hard to recover from here because there is a pseudo remedy: his behavior changes. Plus, he does not have to change his tech habits. It's a win-win for parents and children. The parent gets the pragmatic, optimal desired behavior, and the child does not have to give up his addictive behavior. One of the most effective solutions to this problem is a curfew of screen time in the evening, if not amputation altogether (Matthew 5:30). There are other issues with blue light, like macular degeneration, a common eye impairment for the older generation. As much as I thank God for tablets where I can access and read fantastic Christ-centered content, I'm also aware that I'm putting my eyes in harm's way. I don't want to be like the twenty-five-year-old smoker who does not believe he can get cancer.

Call to Action

1. Why is the blue light effect a real and tragic phenomenon?
2. What does descriptive psychology mean, and why does it provide no long-term, heart-transforming solutions?
3. Why do parents prefer medications because it's more about the performance of the child than addressing the uniqueness of the child?
4. What would tech moderation or amputation mean to you and your child?
5. How does the fear of man hinder you from making the right tech decisions for those you love? If fear of man is a factor, how do you plan to change?

7

Accountability
Effect

These adverse cyber effects always beg the question of the best time to give your child a phone. Part of the discussion centers on the type of phone you want to give your child. The other part centers on the kind of child you have, their maturity level, or if God has regenerated them. You also want to consider their personalities. Some children are leaders and not easily influenced; others are followers, easily tempted, or have dull to hard consciences. It could be a practical choice if you want your child to have a flip phone at an early age. If it's a smartphone, you need to make a few sober assessments about the maturity level of your child and the accessibility options that you want to give them. If your child has to have a smartphone because all his peers have one, you will feed his pre-existing addiction if you give him one. The addiction is peer pressure, codependency, or what the Bible calls the fear of man (Proverbs 29:25).

Is it wise to give your child a phone so he won't feel out-of-step with his peer group? It's illogical. If his peers were using drugs, would you buy him weed so he can fit in? Do you want to provide him a false god where his ability to feel good about himself connects to his phone, not the Sovereign

Lord? Wouldn't it be better to identify and isolate the heart idolatry and teach him how he can have a bigger God while bringing his friends down a notch or two? Wouldn't it be better that he does not succumb to the control of what he or his friends have? Don't feed his addiction, but help him to overcome the desire so he can be Christlike. He may "hate" you now, but he will love you later, especially if the Lord gets hold of his heart.

The best time to give a son (or daughter) a smartphone is when he is mature enough to resist the temptation of porn. When you know that pornography is not an issue in his mind or life, you can think about giving him a device that is one click away from more sexually explicit content than any generation before him could imagine or access. The best time to give your daughter (or son) a smartphone is when she does not have to be on social media. She's not interested in those platforms, what they offer, and how they suck you into the black hole of false intimacy. If she had instead wanted to build real-world relationships, she's in a great place, and it would be unwise to put anything in her path that would deter this good desire. If she would rather relate in cyberspace than in the real world, you have a problem that may need outside intervention.

Call to Action

1. Does your child have a phone? What are the biblical grounds for giving him or her one?
2. Describe the maturity and personality of your child and how providing a phone would help them mature while giving them a Christlike personality.
3. Why is peer pressure so intense at a young age, what is the solution, and how is giving a phone to a child struggling with fear of man a good idea?
4. What about the fear of man of the parent? Do you need to address your fear of disappointing your child? If so, why does your kid have that kind of power over you?
5. What would be a biblical reason to put something so tempting before a child that could easily entice them into a lifetime of addiction and relational dysfunction?

8

Migration Effect

The global effect of all these issues on the body of Christ is what it's doing to our local churches. The family is the core of all civil societies, and within the Christian world, the family constitutes the local church. In former generations, the social center of every community was the local church building, the structure where Christian families gathered to build koinonia practically. All roads led to the church building. It's where people worshipped, got married, were buried, and gathered socially. We met for choir practice, evangelism, and family fun days. We coined an expression to emphasize the value of the building: "We're going to church." We let the Internet age destroy the historical, social center for the Christian community. We have migrated to endless social communities in cyberspace, relocating the church building to the perimeter of our lives and moving our preferred social media platforms to the center.

We have thrown the baby out with the bathwater as we mock our former "three to thrive habits" of showing up for church Sunday morning, Sunday night, and Wednesday night. We restricted our church attendance sermon diet to once on Sunday, competing with our vacations, Sundays on the lake, and kid's sports. Meanwhile, our youth have full access to these social platforms where they can hang out with their friends anytime, day or night, and they love it. When they turn eighteen and go to college or get jobs, it's not a big deal for many of them to leave their local churches behind because the building (or its inhabitants, the church) was not at the center of their lives anyhow; it was one of many social offerings that sat on the perimeter. I mean, "Why get in a car and drive to the building to meet up with someone when I can do it in seconds online?"

A high view of the church, which was a given, is old-school. There are several reasons why our teens are leaving our churches in droves, but you will always find a smartphone and its effects associated with this problem. One of the assessment questions you want to ask about your child is his view of the local church. Is he committed to it, as evidenced by his desire to fellowship with flesh and blood people in the church? Or would his first impulse be to grab his phone and connect there? Are you committed to your local church? Or do you prefer strangers on the train, in cyberspace, or some other spot where connecting is more effortless, but transformative, sanctifying, discipleship is lacking?

Call to Action

1. Why might bringing back the three-to-thrive, old-school practice be better?
2. What would you have to change to unhook from social media and reconnect with your local church family?
3. What if you committed to Sunday morning and one other weekly church meeting, e.g., a small group? What would you need to change? How would you benefit?
4. Perhaps you've enabled your child to drift from the church by creating a new social epicenter for him through his technology. Will you discuss this with your child if it's true for you?
5. What must you do to create, re-establish, or enhance a high view of the church in your life?

Summing Up

The cyber effect is real. Though we won't understand it entirely, we have enough data to respond differently than our culture. We are redemptive agents doing the Lord's work. The devil has thrown us a massive curveball, but we can take it, reverse it, and use it redemptively. The question for us is whether or not we believe this is a big enough problem that needs our attention and intentionality.

1. If you do, then what will you do? What will you change about how you use technology? What changes do you need to make right now, and what is your specific plan to change the tech culture within your sphere of influence?
2. Will you review the questions I have asked you throughout this book with a friend, making adjustments as needed?

About the Author

Rick Thomas launched the Life Over Coffee global training network in 2008 to bring hope and help for you and others by creating resources that spark conversations for transformation. His primary responsibilities are resource creation and leadership development, which he does through speaking, writing, podcasting, and educating. In 1990 he earned a BA in Theology and, in 1991, a BS in Education. In 1993, he received his ordination into Christian ministry, and in 2000, he graduated with an MA in Counseling from The Master's University. In 2006, he was recognized as a Fellow of the Association of Certified Biblical Counselors (ACBC).

Other Books Available from
Life Over Coffee

Boasting in Weakness
Centering Your Marriage on Christ
Communication
Complete Marriage
Don't Apologize
Exchange the Truth for a Lie
Help My Marriage Has Grown Cold
Identity Crisis
Local Church
Loving Me
Mad
Marriage Devotion We Are One
Politics and Culture
Parenting Devotion from Zero to Adulthood
Sex, Temptation, and Modesty
Storm Hurler
The Cyber Effect
The Talk
Wives Leading
You Decide